ASTONISHING ART with RECYCLED RUBBISH

Crafty creations
Reduce, reuse, recycle!

Susan Martineau

Illustrated by Martin Ursell

b small publishing
www.bsmall.co.uk

Contents

Before You Begin

Start a rubbish collection! All kinds of old junk can be transformed into amazing artwork.

Make sure the rubbish is clean and dry before you store it. Boxes can be folded flat so they take up less room when stored.

Don't forget to use old newspapers to cover work surfaces before you begin a project. To protect your clothes you could wear an old shirt back to front. Old detergent bottle caps make great containers for paints and glue.

Don't get too carried away collecting rubbish – stop when you have a boxful and get cracking on some of the ideas in this book.

You will need a bit of grown-up help in one or two places. These have been marked with this special symbol.

!

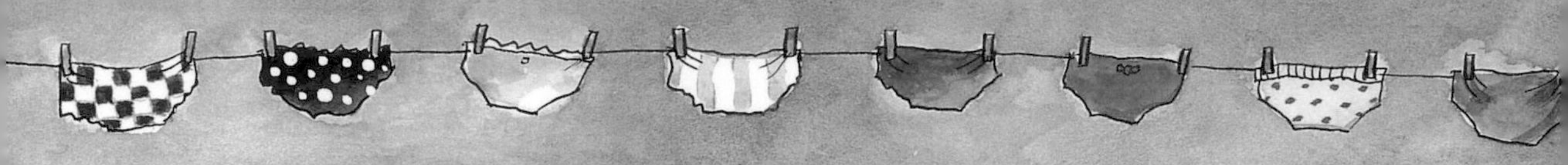

The Original Bum Bag

Don't throw away underwear that doesn't fit any more. Make yourself the ultimate in recycled accessories!

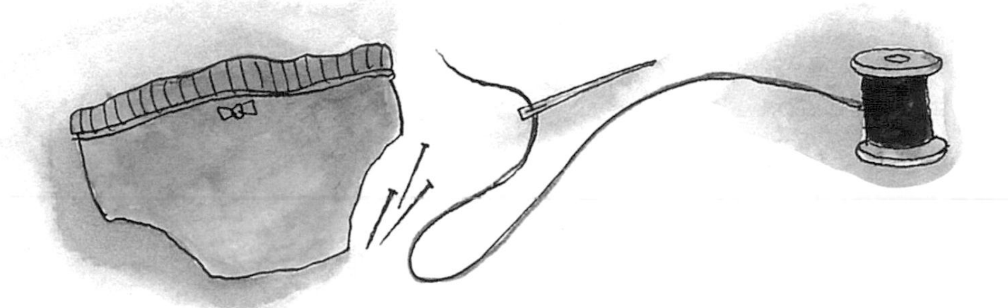

What you will need:

- 1 pair of old, clean, coloured underpants or knickers
- pins
- needle and coloured thread
- old school name tapes or old ribbon
- 3 buttons, same or assorted, at least 2 cm across
- 3 old hair elastics
- belt for wearing the bag

Hold the edges of the leg holes together. Pin and sew closed. Knot thread when finished.

Fold the gusset of the pants up inside and oversew closed. Trim off the gusset flap inside.

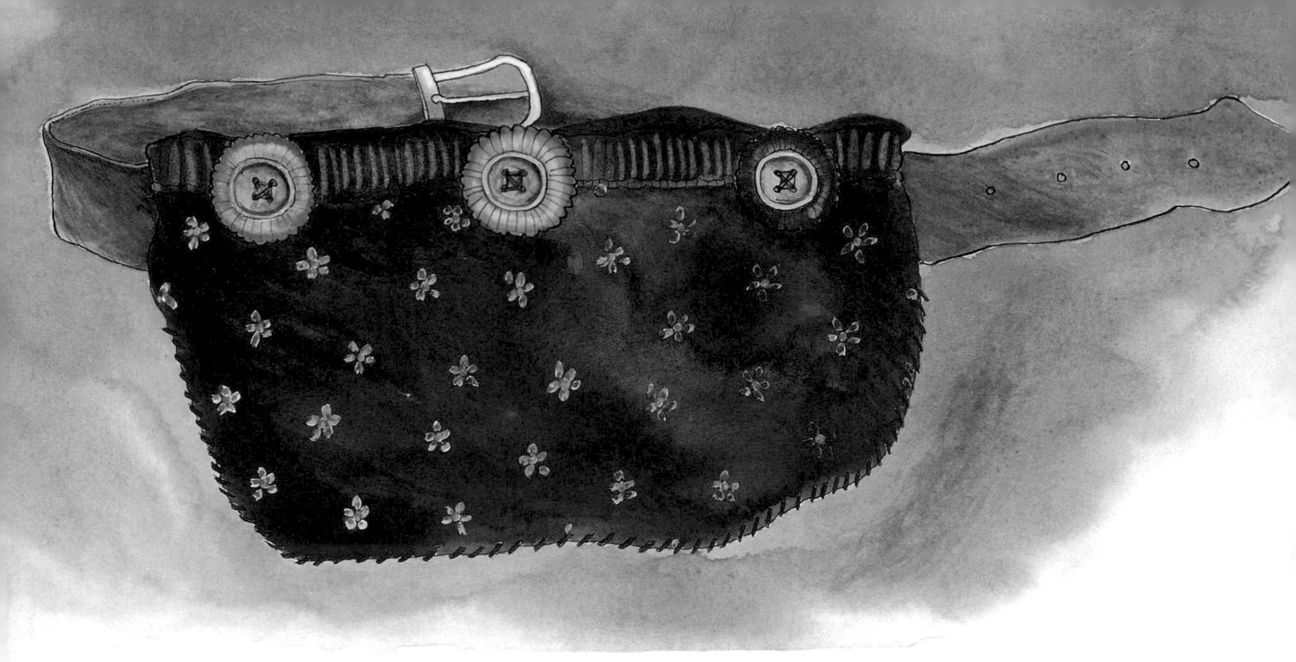

Turn the pants over and sew on the name tapes or short lengths of ribbon. These are the belt loops.

Sew the buttons next to the waistband at the front of the pants.

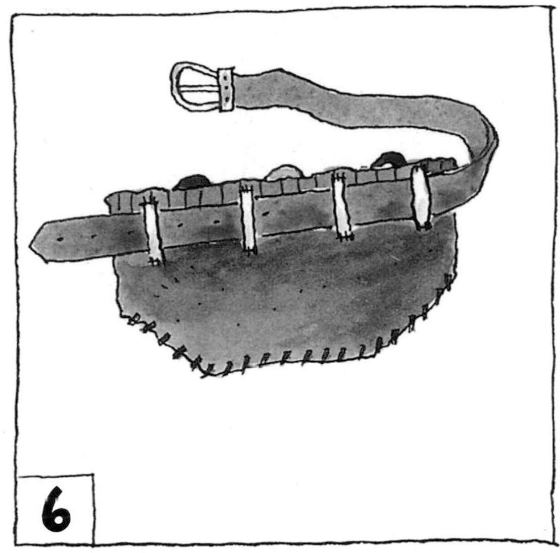

On the back waistband, line up the hair elastics with the buttons. Sew them on. Use them to close the bum bag.

Your bum bag is ready for action. Just slide a belt through the loops and put it on!

THINK ABOUT IT!

Well-to-do medieval and Tudor folk had a very good use for their old clothes. They cut them into handy little pieces to be used as loo paper!

Self-portrait with Rubbish

Make a truly original portrait of yourself. You'll need some of your old clothes that don't fit any more. You could make portraits of your entire family or some friends too.

What you will need:

- very large cardboard box
- pencil
- scissors
- a complete set of old clothes, e.g. tracksuit, T-shirt, socks, etc.
- plastic carrier bags (brown, yellow, black or orange, depending on your hair colour)
- sticky tape
- an old cork
- felt-tip pens
- glue
- brown or black wool or old hair elastics
- red or pink wool or old hair elastics
- old pencil rubber

Open up the box and spread it out flat. Lie down on it and ask a friend to draw around your outline with a pencil.

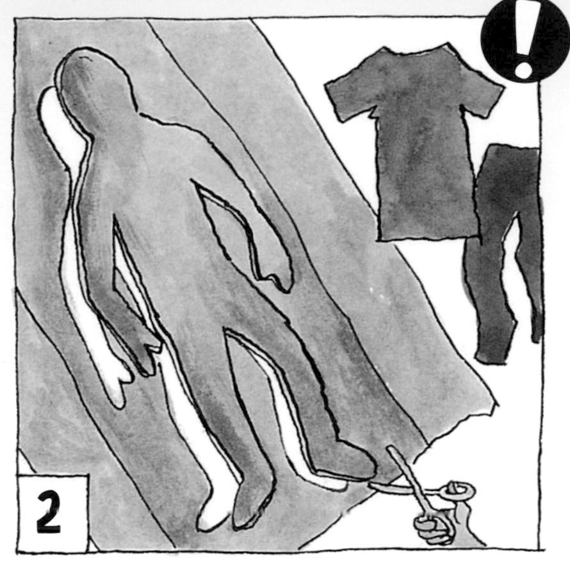

Cut out your cardboard self and dress it in your old clothes.

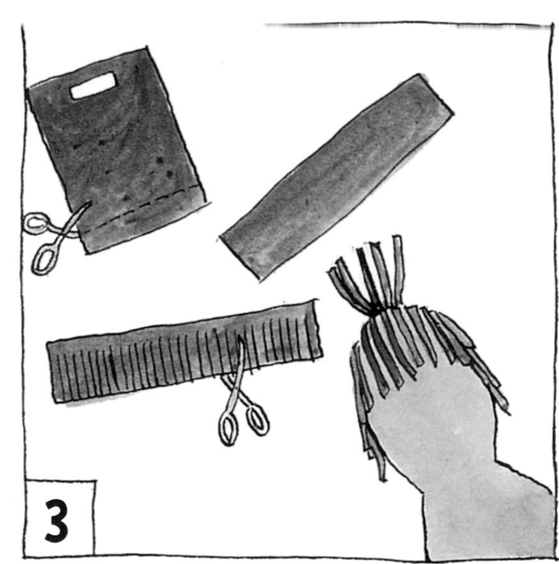

Cut strips of carrier bag. Snip them into fringes for hair. Tape on to the head. Trim to suit your style!

Create Your Face

☆☆☆☆☆ Portrait Party ☆☆☆☆☆

Throw a portrait party and get all your friends to make portraits of each other or themselves.

Ask everyone to start collecting useful junk for this a few weeks beforehand. They'll also need to bring their own very large box. If you can do the portraits in a garden or park you'll all have enough room to be creative!

Wacky Weaving

How many plastic carrier bags have you got lurking around your house? You could transform some of them into this nifty woven bag. You will need to repeat steps 1 and 2 to make two pieces of weaving.

What you will need:

- 3 different-coloured plastic carrier bags, cut into 3-cm wide strips
- medium-sized cardboard box
- scissors
- sticky tape

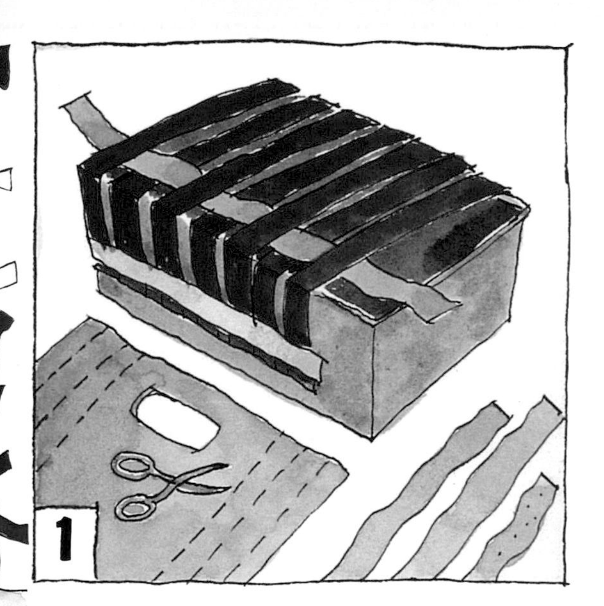

Tape strips of one colour across the box. Weave strips of the other colours in and out across the box in the other direction.

Put tape across all the edges of the woven area. Remove from box. Turn over and tape the other side. Repeat steps 1 and 2 to make two pieces.

Tape the two pieces of weaving together to form a bag.
Snip the fringes into thinner strands.

Plait three strips of plastic.
Knot each end to finish.
Tape inside bag to form strap.

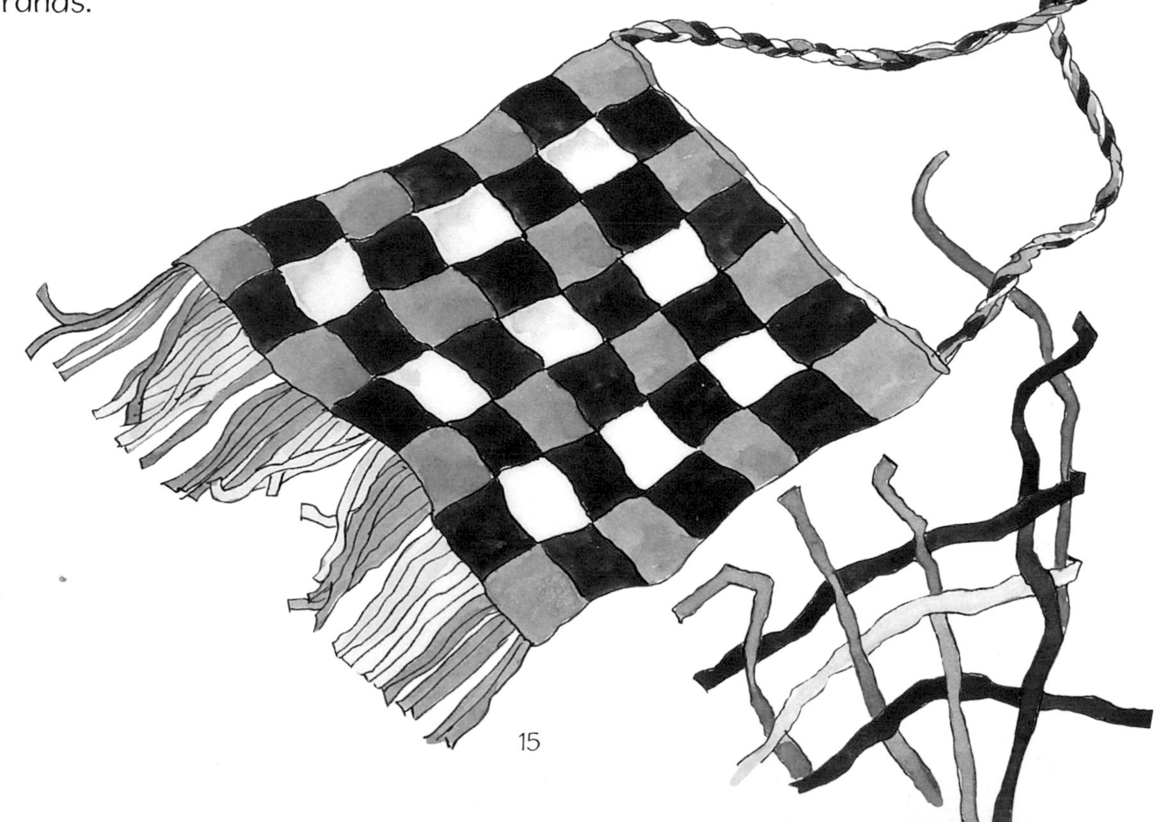

Onion Fish

Old onion skins make fantastic fish scales. Collect just the top layer of brown onion skin – you'll see that it's beautifully shiny inside. You could make a whole aquarium!

What you will need:

- coloured paper (blue is good)
- pencil
- onion skins
- scissors
- glue
- an old cork or some plain white card
- black felt-tip pen

1

Lightly draw one or more fish outlines on the paper.

2

Trim pieces of onion skin to shape for fins, tail and head. Glue them in position, shiny side up.

Cut scales and glue them on, shiny side up. Start from the tail and overlap them.

Cut a slice of cork or circle of card for the eye. Draw a pupil in the middle with the felt-tip. Glue in position.

Big Box Croc

Leave this cardboard critter lying around to surprise your friends. He can be as big as you like – the bigger the better. You can use all those boxes you have been collecting for a rainy day.

What you will need:

- about 8 (or more) assorted rectangular or square boxes, e.g. shoeboxes, tissue boxes, teabag boxes, long thin boxes used for packing bottles
- 5 egg-boxes
- card from cereal box or similar
- glue
- sticky tape
- thick paint (green, white, yellow, black)
- paintbrushes
- string
- scissors
- metal skewer
- pencil

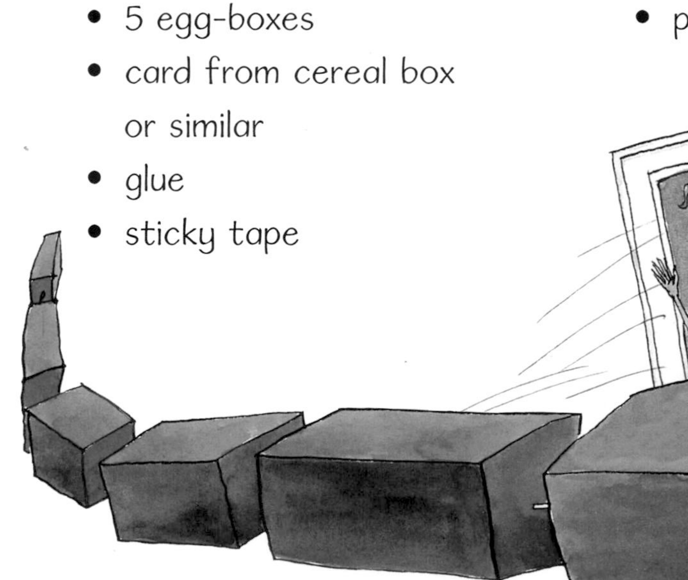

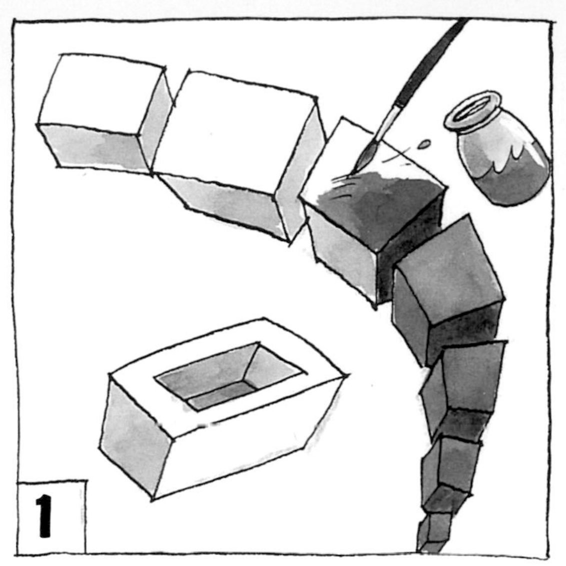

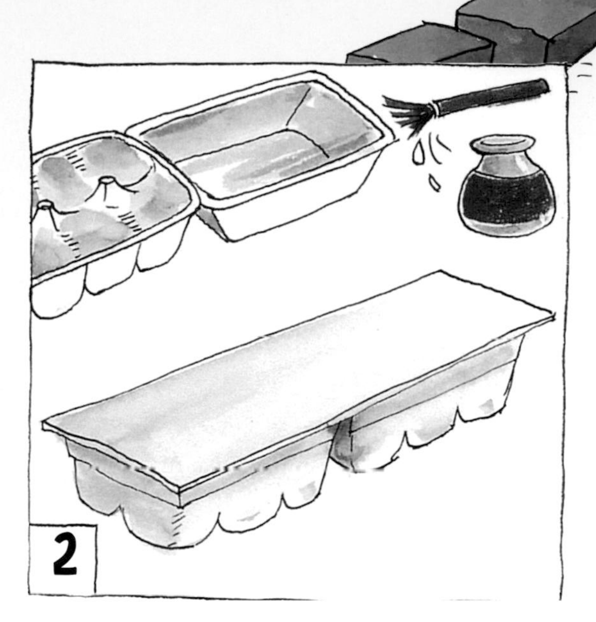

For the body: lay all the boxes in a line, with the thinnest ones at the tail. Remove the lids or cut a hole in each box, so you can put your hand inside. Paint all the boxes green. Leave them to dry.

For the head: glue two of the egg-boxes shut. Lay them end to end and cut a rectangle of card to cover the top. Glue it in place.

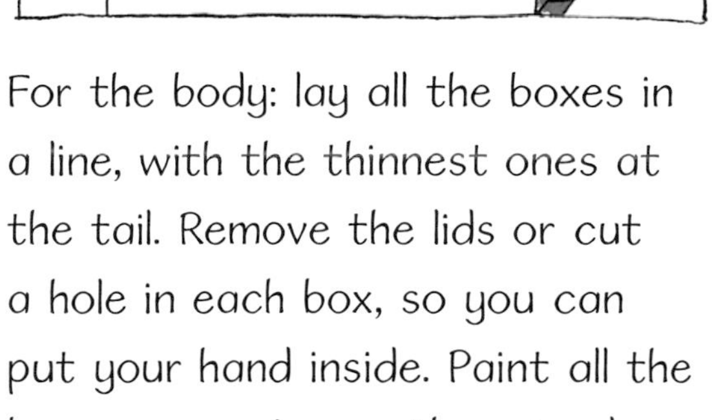

Repeat step 2 with two more egg-boxes. Cut two cups from the last egg-box. Glue them to the top of one head section.

Paint the teeth white and the rest of the head green. Leave to dry, then glue the two head sections together. Paint two yellow eyes with black pupils.

THINK ABOUT IT!

Crocodiles have been around for nearly 200 million years, but they're now endangered because the swamplands and rainforests they live in are being destroyed. Hunters also killed about 10 million crocodiles between 1870 and 1970 to make belts, shoes, bags and wallets from their skins.

With the skewer, make a small hole in each end of all the boxes. Thread a short length of string between each box and the next. Knot the ends inside.

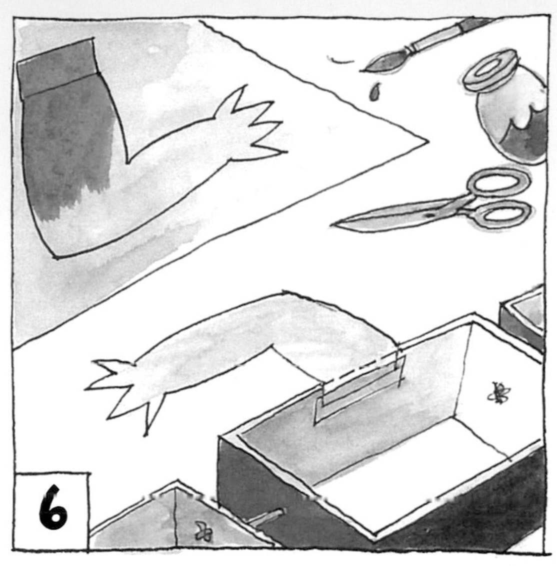

Draw two pairs of legs on the card. Paint green, leave to dry, then cut out. Fold a small flap at the end of each limb. Tape firmly inside the body boxes.

Masterful Masks

Elephant Ears

A very simple idea which just uses old egg-boxes and card.

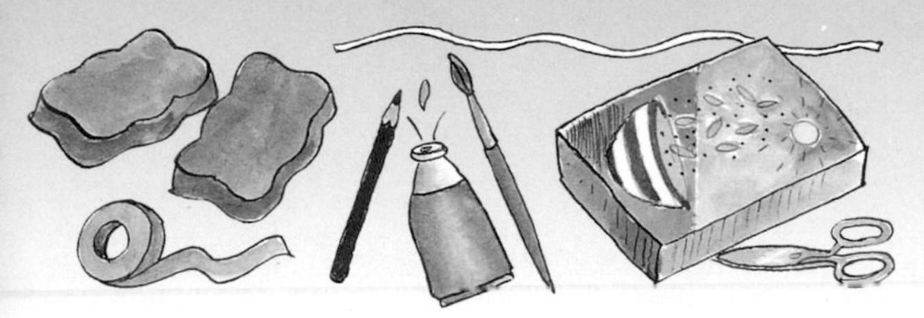

What you will need:

- 2 egg-box lids
- grey paint and paintbrush
- scissors
- sticky tape
- thin card from cereal box or similar
- pencil
- elastic

First paint the lids grey. (Some egg-boxes are already grey so this may not be necessary.)

Cut two eye holes in one lid. Cut away one edge, as shown, to make the head shape and start of the trunk.

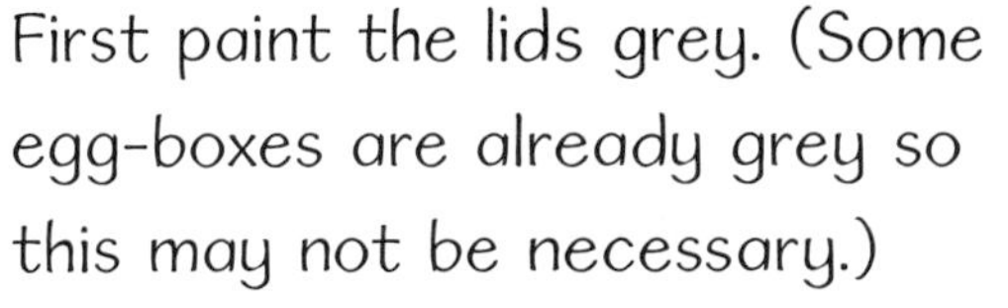

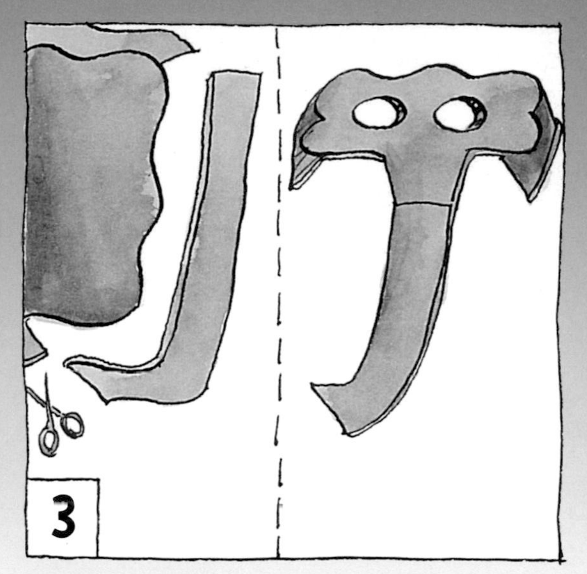

Cut a strip from along one side and corner of the other lid to make a trunk. Tape to the head.

Draw two ear shapes on the card. Cut out and tape to the side of the head with the grey side facing out.

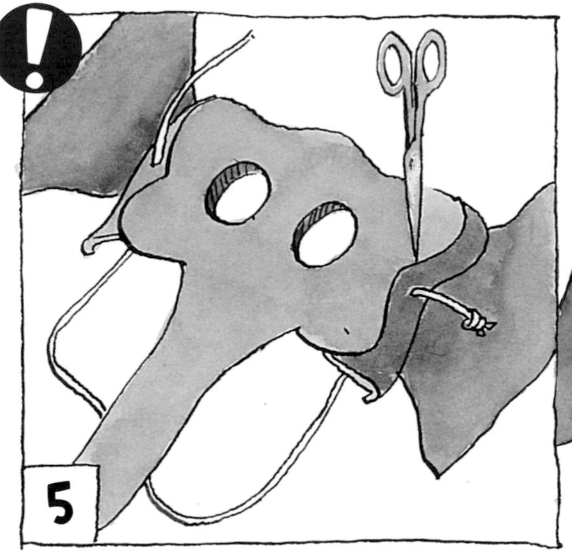

Make a hole in each side of the head with the point of the scissors. Thread through elastic and knot to finish.

Foxy Features

Make a cheeky foxy face using card and old sponges. You could also try out other animals – rabbits, badgers, bears – using the same basic idea.

What you will need:

- card from cereal box or similar
- pencil
- scissors
- wax crayons
- toilet roll tube
- old, clean sponge (yellow, orange or white)
- glue
- elastic

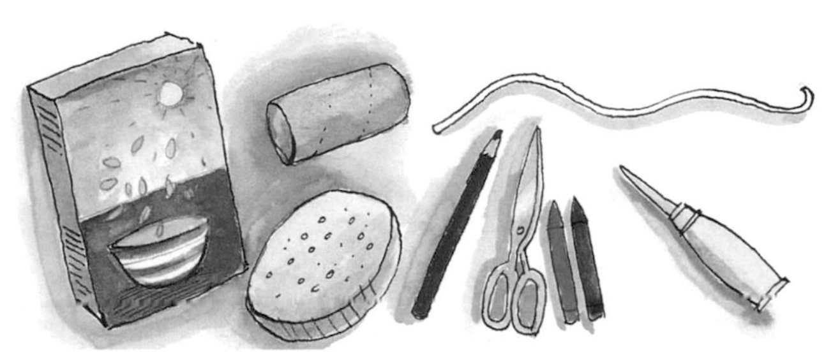

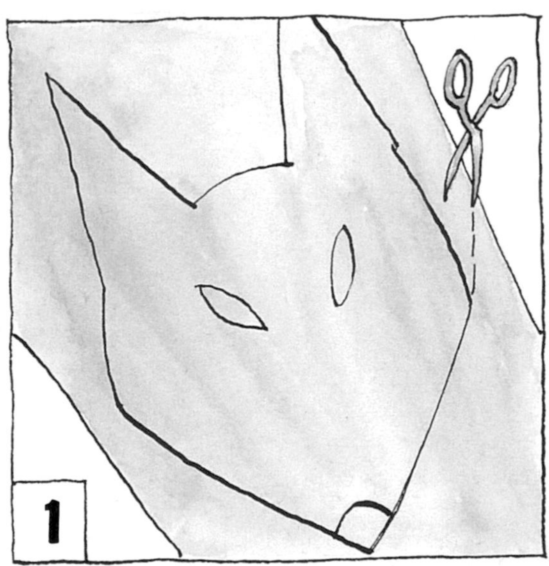

Draw a simple fox face on the card. Cut it out. Cut two slanting eye holes. Colour the face orange with a black nose.

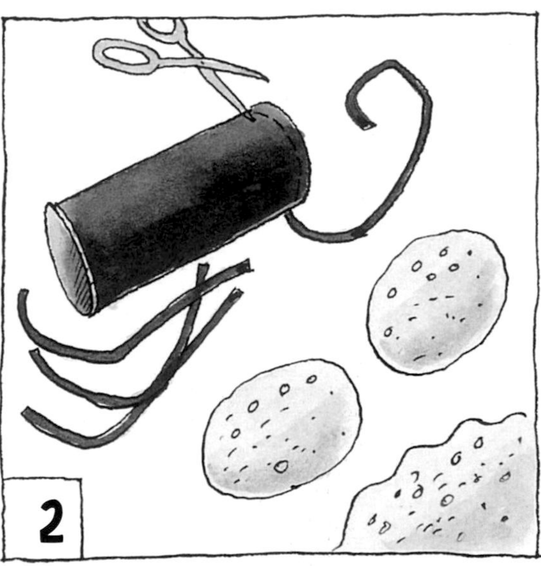

Colour the toilet roll tube black. Cut six very thin strands for whiskers. Cut two small cheeks from sponge.

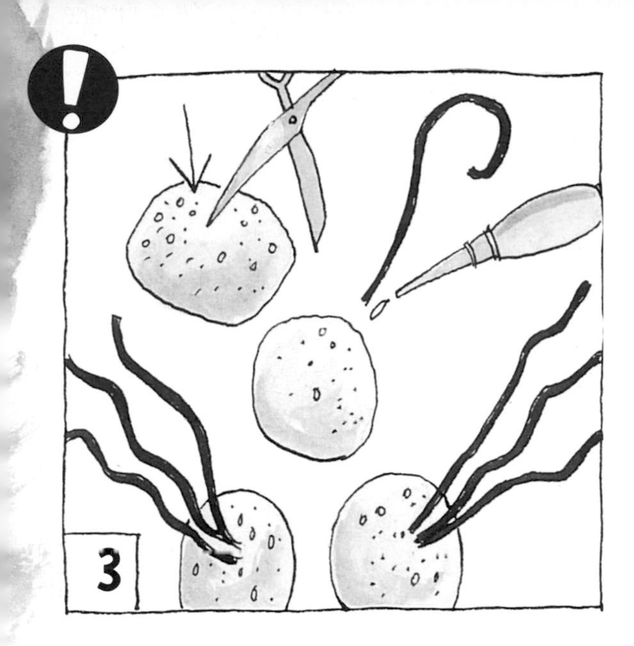

Make a hole in each sponge. Dab glue at the end of each whisker, and push three into each cheek.

Glue the cheeks on to the face. Make two holes for the elastic. Thread through and knot to finish.

Crazy Cuttings

The perfect way to use up old, unwanted family photos once the best ones are in the album. Recycle those old postcards and magazines that are gathering dust too.

What you will need:

- old family photos, especially ones including your mugshot
- old fan magazines (sports or music)
- old postcards
- scissors
- glue

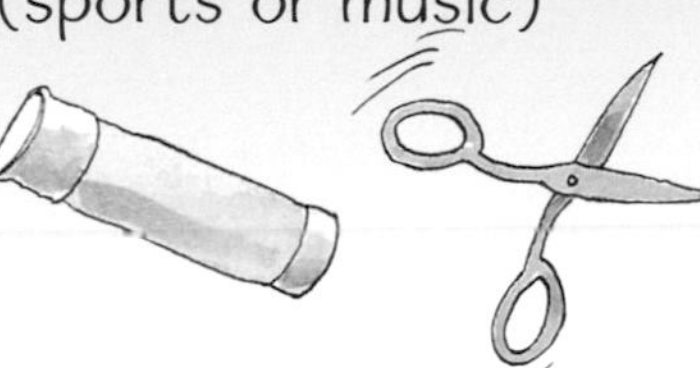

WARNING!
Please make sure the photos are not prized family portraits before you start hacking into them!

Cut out the heads from the photos. Trim to remove as much background as possible.

Sift through postcards for scenes with people in them. Sort through the magazines to find your favourite stars.

Now start placing the photo heads on top of the heads in the postcards and magazine pictures to see which ones look best!

Glue them in place. Cut out the magazine pictures.

☆☆☆☆☆ You're Framed! ☆☆☆☆☆

You could make a simple frame from old pieces of card.

Paint card pieces, or cover them with old wrapping paper or foil. Glue together on three sides only. Leave one side open to slide in your star creation.

THINK ABOUT IT!

Most paper collected for recycling is made into ... more paper – everything from elegant stationery to toilet paper and cardboard boxes. But amazingly it may also end up as fuel, building materials, cars, shoes or even kitty litter!

You can stick your sneaky pictures on your wall or send them to a friend. Autograph your 'fan' shots and personalize with a message from the famous 'you'.

Jurassock Park

Create your own dinosaurs out of old socks and scourers. The following are just some ideas to get you started. You can make up your own prehistoric pets too.

What you will need:

- clean old socks, any size or colour but black, green, grey and brown are best
- ordinary or fluorescent felt-tip pens
- toilet roll tube
- scissors
- used but clean washing-up sponges and scourers
- needle and thread
- old red or pink ribbon

Put the sock on your hand, with your thumb in the heel. Draw eyes and nostrils in felt-tip pen.

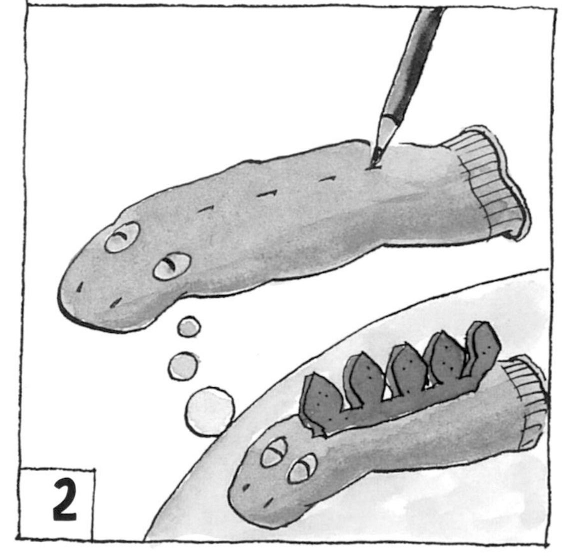

Make small felt-tip marks where you would like to position spines, horns, and other features.

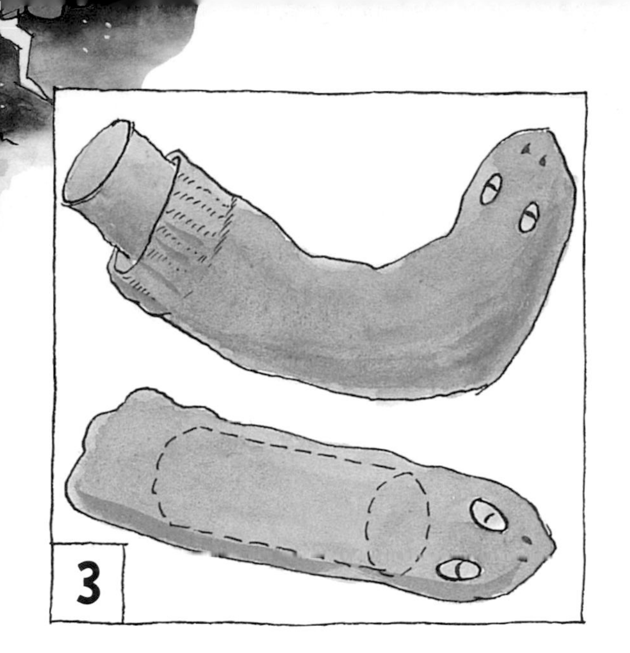

Take off the sock and push the toilet roll tube inside it to stop you from sewing right through the sock.

You could paint a prehistoric poster to use as a background for your dino puppets.

Top Triceratops

Cut a frill out of a large, stiff, green pan scourer. Cut three horns from the same scourer.

Sew into position using simple running stitches.

Stegosockus

Cut two rows of bony plates out of a stiff scourer. Sew in position.

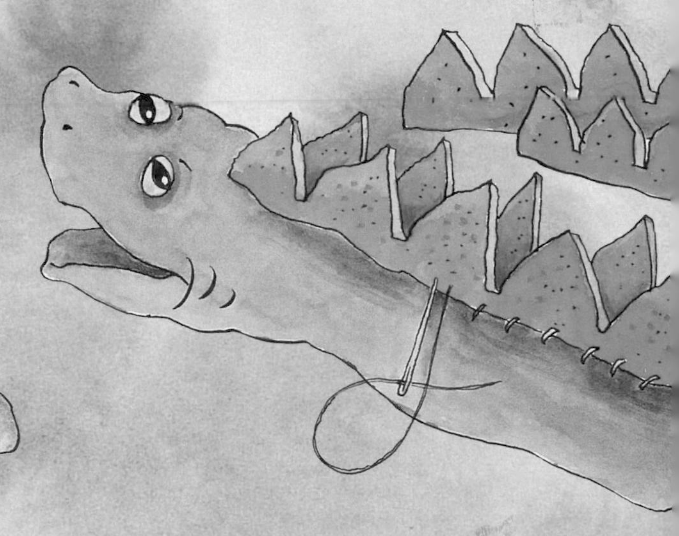

Mighty Meat-eater

Cut some rows of teeth out of a sponge scourer and stitch them inside the mouth. Cut a tongue out of ribbon and stitch in position.

☆☆☆☆ Puppet Pets ☆☆☆☆

Socks can be made into all kinds of weird and amazing puppet creatures. Just look at your rubbish collection and see what else you can use: old wool, string or strips of plastic carrier bag for fur or a mane; can pulls for scales; beads and buttons for eyes.

On Guard!

Save up as much old, cleaned tinfoil as you can to make your own medieval armour.

Shiny Shield

Add your own personal emblem to finish your shield.

What you will need:

- large piece of cardboard
- pencils and scissors
- old, clean tinfoil
- sticky tape
- old ribbons, coloured card or old glitzy wrapping paper

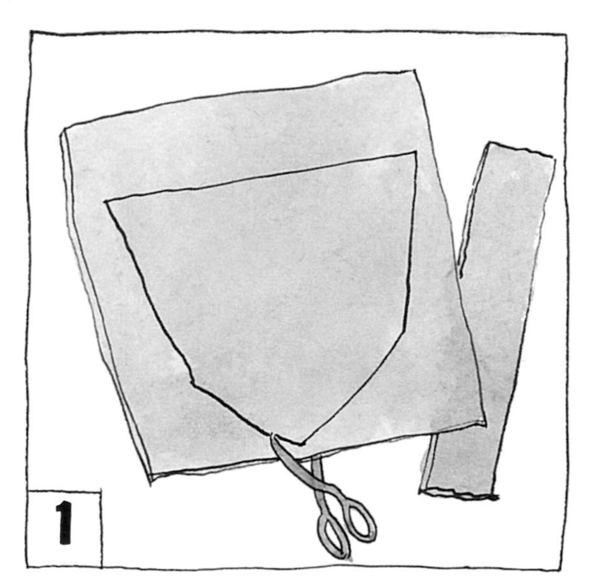

Draw the outline of your shield on the cardboard. Cut it out. Cut out a wide strip of cardboard.

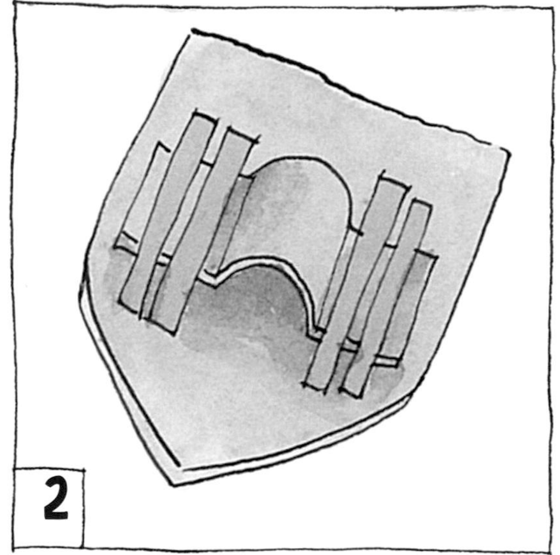

Tape the strip on to the back of the shield as shown, leaving space for your hand.

Cover the front of the shield with pieces of tinfoil. Sticky tape doesn't show up on tinfoil, so it doesn't matter how many pieces you have to use.

Design your own emblem. Use the ribbon, card or wrapping paper in any combination you like.

Short Sword

If you find a large enough piece of card you can make this into a long jousting sword instead!

What you will need:

- thick cardboard
- pencil
- scissors
- old, clean foil dish
- old, clean tinfoil
- sticky tape

Draw the shape of the sword blade on the cardboard. Cut it out.

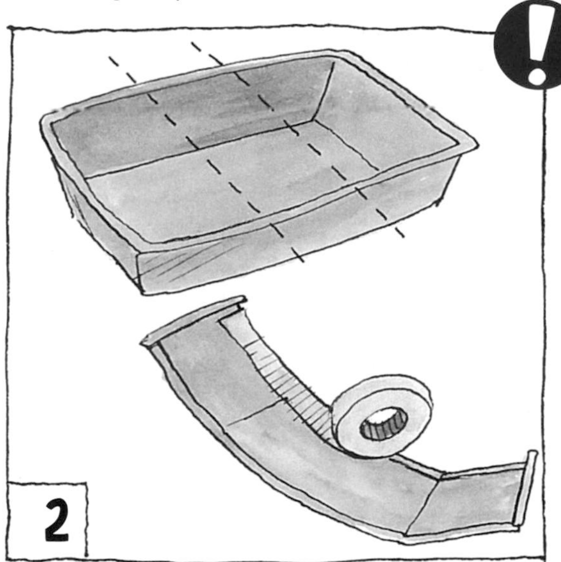

Cut a wide strip from the foil dish. Fold over and tape along the cut edges.

Cover the blade with tinfoil. Cut a slit in the middle of the foil strip and slot the blade through. Fix with sticky tape. Curve the strip to form the sword hilt.

THINK ABOUT IT!

Medieval muck left behind in the ancient rubbish pits of castles can give us a brilliant picture of what life might have been like then. For example, animal bones tell us what people ate.

Megga Mosaics

You can make mosaics from all kinds of rubbish – just look at your collection of stuff and try out different materials. Simple patterns, flags and heraldic emblems all make great designs. You could make yourself a mosaic bedroom nameplate.

Terracotta Eggshells

Collect empty eggshells from cooking or from boiled-egg meals. Wash them out and leave to dry. Six half shells will be enough to makc a picture about 16 cm long and 14 cm wide.

What you will need:

- clean eggshells
- different-coloured paints
- paintbrushes
- paper
- pencil
- glue

You don't need to paint right to the edge of the shells.

1

Paint some of the eggshells different colours. Leave to dry. Leave some shells unpainted.

Draw your design lightly on the paper in pencil. Decide where you want each colour to go.

Break off bits of shell and apply glue. Press into position. The eggshell will crack, but the inside 'skin' will hold it together.

☆☆☆☆☆☆☆☆☆☆☆☆☆☆

The Finishing Touch

☆☆☆☆☆☆☆☆☆☆☆☆☆☆

Varnish your mosaic for a real glazed look. Mix 1 teaspoon of PVA glue with 3 teaspoons of water and brush lightly across the mosaic.. It will become clear when dry.

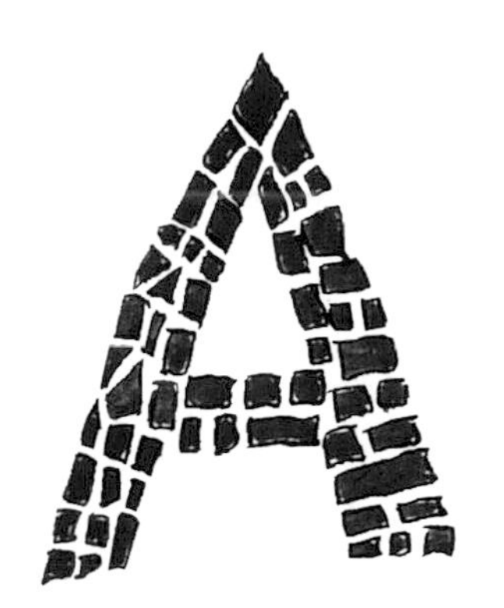

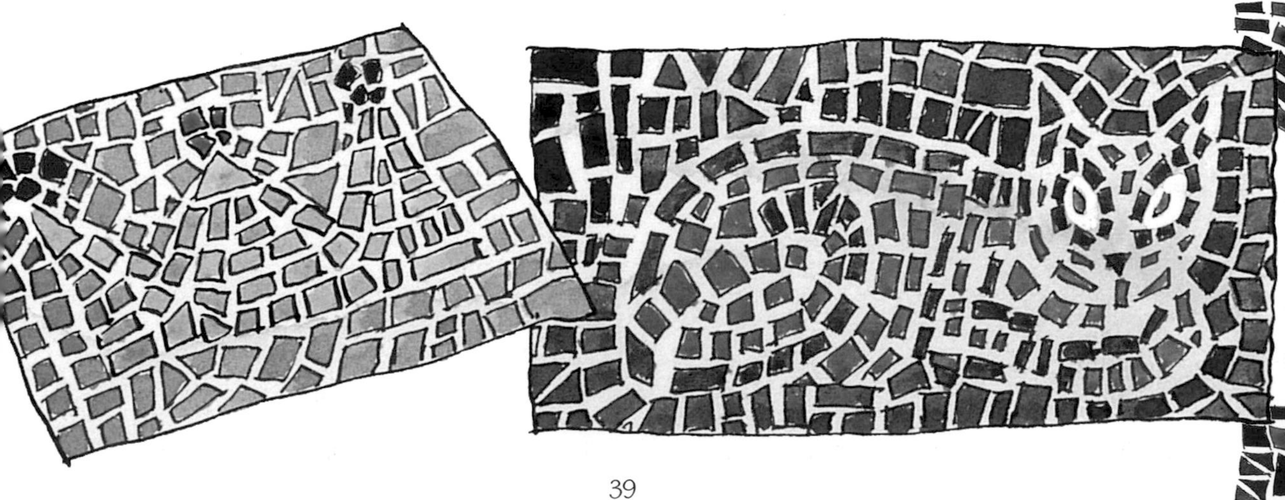

Magazine Mosaic

Sort through old magazines and catalogues and look for solid blocks of colour. You will need about four different colours to work with. Slightly different shades of the same colour are fine. Clothes catalogues are really good for solid areas of one colour.

What you will need:

- old magazines or catalogues
- scissors and glue
- plain paper and pencil
- old envelopes or plastic pots to keep coloured squares separate

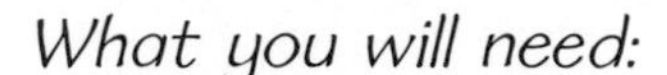

1

Cut out solid areas of your chosen colours and trim down to 1-cm squares. Keep each colour in a separate envelope or pot.

2

Draw your design in pencil first. Then plan where you want your colours to go.

Glue a small area of the outline at a time and fill in with squares. Where whole squares will not fit, cut them to fill the space.

THINK ABOUT IT!

Roman public lavatories were often decorated with mosaics, and dolphin designs were very popular. At the Roman loos in Timgad, in North Africa, carved dolphin armrests were even placed between each seat!

Fit for a Pharaoh

This is really royal rubbish and guaranteed to impress your friends.

Jewelled Collar

Ask your friends to help you collect loads of can pulls. You will need as many different colours as possible for the jewels!

What you will need:

- an old T-shirt (any colour)
- coloured pencils and paper
- pinking shears
- can pulls
- needle and thread

1

Draw the outline of the collar on the T-shirt. Cut it out with pinking shears.

2

Place lines of can pulls in a pattern on the front of the collar. Copy your design on a piece of paper.

Sew the can pulls on to the collar with a simple running stitch. To wear the collar, just pull it on over your head.

Amulet Armlet

Wear this embossed armlet on your upper arm in true Ancient Egyptian style. The eye design is the Eye of Horus – the protective sign of the sky god! Try some designs of your own.

What you will need:

- 1 toilet roll tube
- scissors
- thick string or old shoelace
- glue
- old tinfoil (silver or gold, but clean)

THINK ABOUT IT!

Unfortunately Ancient Egyptian mummies have not always been treated with respect. Ground-up mummy used to be made into medicines during the sixteenth and seventeenth centuries.

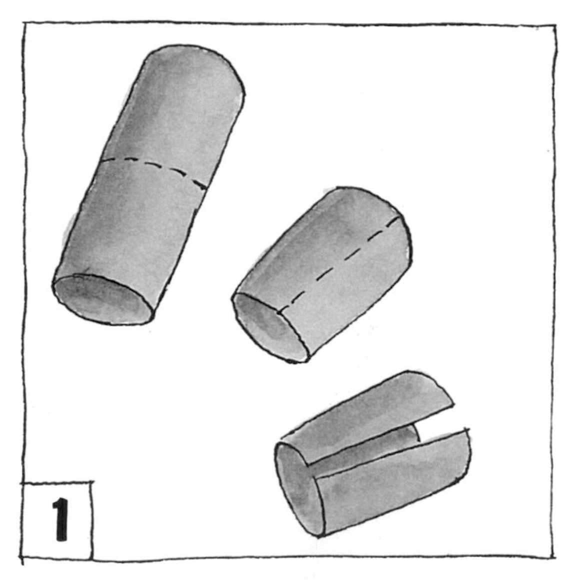

Cut the tube in half. Make a vertical cut up one of the halves.

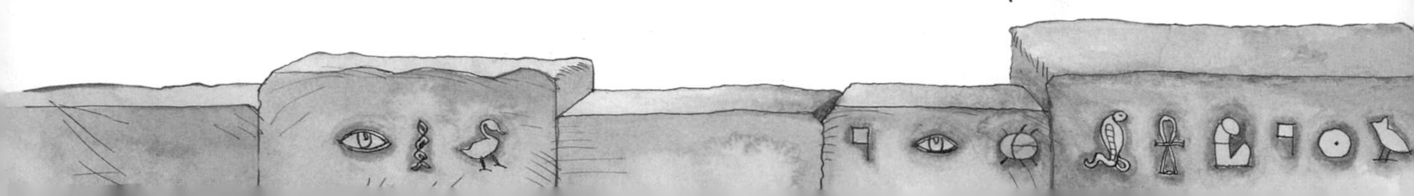

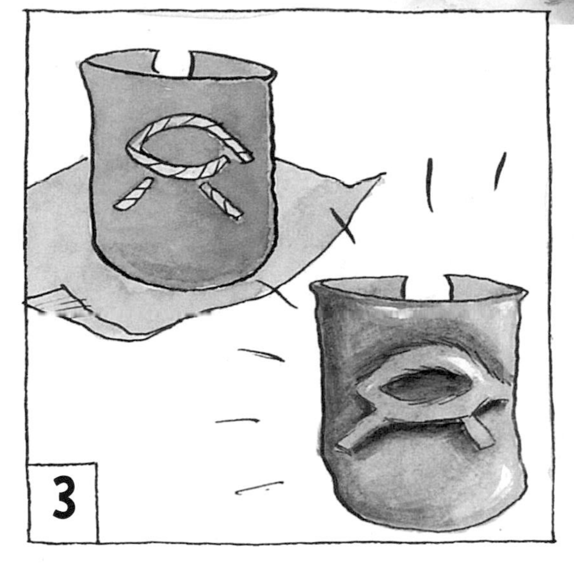

Glue on pieces of string or shoelace in an eye design as shown. Let it dry.

Carefully cover the tube with a piece of foil. Gently press around the eye design.

The Great Rubbish Race

A daft game for two or more players. The loser gets a wonderful, mucky surprise! This is definitely one for outdoors.

Each player has to walk the course in bare feet. Everyone else closes their eyes and listens. The player must try not to rustle, clank, or squeal with disgust. Whoever is noisiest has to get inside the bin bag and jump along the course to gather up the rubbish afterwards.

What you will need:

- old newspapers
- 9 unsquashed, empty drinks cans
- a few banana skins or a pile of potato, carrot or other vegetable peelings
- several empty crisp packets
- some polystyrene fruit and vegetable trays
- 1 large dustbin bag or plastic refuse sack

THINK ABOUT IT!

We all need to get into the habit of recycling as much as possible. Old junk that you haven't made into amazing artwork can be sorted into different types for recycling bin collections.

You can even hand down your clothes to someone younger than you when you grow out of them. That's recycling too!

three towers of drinks cans. (Leave just a few inches between each one.)
old newspapers
a pile of peelings
polystyrene trays
crisp packets
more newspaper

Published by b small publishing ltd.
The Book Shed, 36 Leyborne Park,
Kew, Richmond, Surrey, TW9 3HA, UK

This new edition published in 2012
1 2 3 4 5

Colour reproduction: Vimnice Printing Press Co. Ltd., Hong Kong
Printed in China by WKT Co. Ltd.
Editorial: Susan Martineau, Olivia Norton and Ronne Randall
Design: Lone Morton and Louise Millar
Production: Madeleine Ehm
ISBN 978-1-908164-61-2
British Library Cataloguing-in-Publication Data.
A catalogue record for this book is available from the British Library.

b small publishing